T0036551

WHERE DO OCEAN CREATURES SLEEP AT NIGHT?

To Ford, Teddy, Georgina, Jack Steven, William, Luke, and the next generation with much love. I hope our oceans and the sea life below remain healthy for you and your children and those who follow.—S. J. S.

To the ones who read me bedtime stories—Dad, Mom, and Shirley—and to the beautiful oceans of our planet and the incredible creatures that inhabit them.—C. R. S.

Keep asking questions, sweet child. Come dive deep with me for answers in this enormous, endlessly beautiful world. Much love to you.—R. E. H.

Where Do Ocean Creatures Sleep at Night?

Steven J. Simmons *and* Clifford R. Simmons

Illustrated by Ruth E. Harper

Charlesbridge

Ocean creatures swim in their watery home.

Near the surface or down deep is where they roam.

When it is time for these animals to rest,

where do they go to sleep their best?

Do they sleep in the open or near a reef?
Or do they swim below rocks and hide underneath?
Let's take a look at what these creatures do
when you are asleep and the day is through.

A stingray glides through the water with wings
and a long tail it can use to sting.
When asleep, a stingray burrows in sand
with its body flat like a large fan.

There it lies hidden, except for its eyes—
to keep watch while it stays in disguise.

An octopus can change the color of its skin
to hide from others as it blends in.
It has many arms—eight to be exact—
and if it loses an arm, a new one grows back!

The octopus can sleep by day or night.
It rests in a hole to stay out of sight.
And when safely sleeping with nothing to fear,
it may still change colors—the reason's not clear!

This creature's head makes it look like a horse.
But it's a fish, so it lives under water, of course!
A seahorse swims upright, unlike most fish;
plants and shrimp are its favorite dish.

When a seahorse sleeps at the end of the day,
it holds a plant or coral so it won't drift away.

A walrus has tusks that are long and white.
If it had to brush them, that would be quite a sight!
It uses its tusks to climb on the ice
and to push away others if they're not acting nice.

A walrus can go for days without rest,
but then it must sleep to be at its best.
It snoozes on land most of the time
but can rest while it's floating—either is fine.

A clownfish can wiggle and do a dance.

It eats tiny animals and also plants.

It lives in anemones that keep away foes;
these homes are poison, and other fish know.
But for the clownfish it's safe to stay,
and here it sleeps at the end of each day.

A bottlenose dolphin can jump very high.

Its long back arches up toward the sky.

It rides waves and plays with friends.

Its mouth seems to smile from end to end.

A dolphin's rest is not very deep,
because only one side of its brain is asleep.
The other side stays awake and aware,
so the dolphin remembers to always breathe air.

A parrotfish has colors that are very bright—
turquoise, red, green, and even some white.
Its teeth are shaped like a parrot's beak,
and that's why its name is so unique.

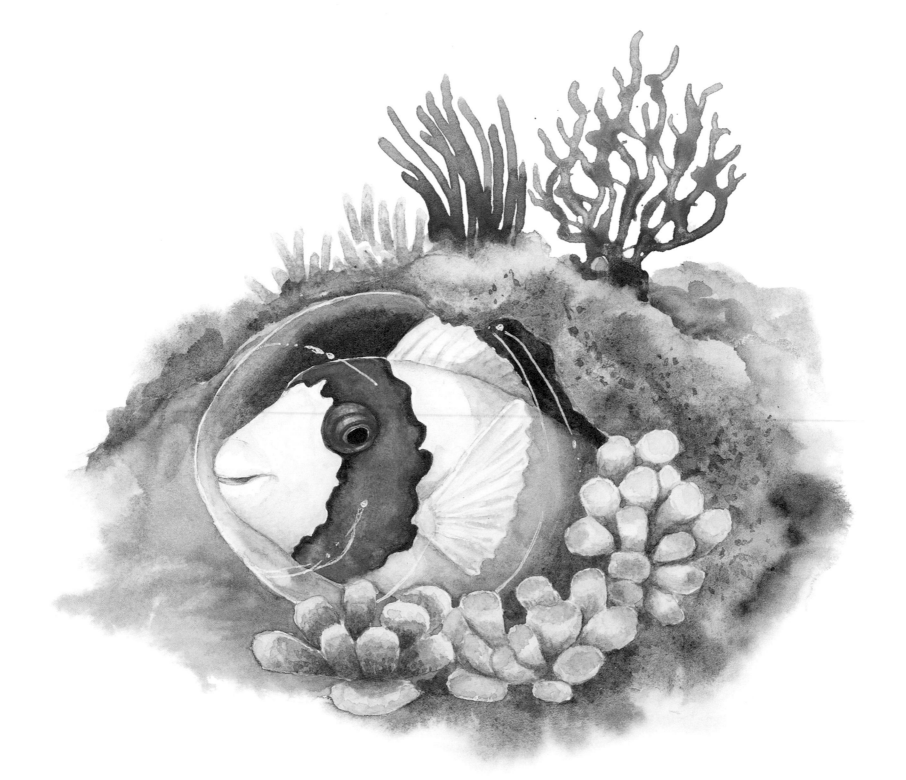

A parrotfish sleeps in a mucus cocoon
that it makes to keep safe in its own gooey room.

A sea turtle has a hard shell on its back
to protect against bites or from an attack.
It stays in warm waters and avoids the cold.
Some live to be more than eighty years old.

When it's time to sleep, a sea turtle will go
either up to the surface or down below.
Under rocks or coral they may tuck away
to rest for several hours a few times a day.

A sea otter looks cuddly and cute,
like it's dressed up in a furry suit.

An otter can rest for hours floating on its back,
using kelp plants as a bed, like a sleep sack.
Otters hold hands so they don't drift afar—
this helps resting otters stay where they are.

One of Earth's biggest creatures is the humpback whale.
Yet it can jump out of the sea with the help of its tail.
A humpback communicates through underwater songs,
and some may last thirty-five minutes long!

This mammal takes naps near the top of the sea.
This is where the sleeping whale must be.
At the surface its blowhole takes in air,
while the whale rests calmly without a care.

The great white shark is fast and strong.
It hunts for food all day long.
Its sharp teeth are a scary sight
and can deliver a powerful bite.

Even a great white needs rest to thrive—
but it must swim while sleeping to stay alive.

Children like you also get wet
in puddles and rain, or your bath—don't forget!
You may go to the beach, a pond, or a pool.
Be sure to play safely while you stay cool.

Then when it's time to rest your head,
you can go to sleep in your nice, dry bed.

GOOD NiGHT!

A note from the authors: Sleep is important for all children. Sleeping gives you the energy you need to grow, learn, laugh, and play. Just as the ocean creatures in this book need sleep to be at their best, so do you!

Text copyright © 2024 by Steven J. Simmons and Clifford R. Simmons
Illustrations copyright © 2024 by Ruth E. Harper
All rights reserved, including the right of reproduction in whole or in part in any form. Charlesbridge and colophon are registered trademarks of Charlesbridge Publishing, Inc.

At the time of publication, all URLs printed in this book were accurate and active. Charlesbridge, the authors, and the illustrator are not responsible for the content or accessibility of any website.

Published by Charlesbridge
9 Galen Street, Watertown, MA 02472
(617) 926-0329 • www.charlesbridge.com

Illustrations done in Daniel Smith watercolors on Arches paper
Display type set in Underland Sans by Wacaksara Co.
Text type set in Museo Slab by Jos Buivenga
Art digitizing and printing by 1010 Printing International Limited in Huizhou, Guangdong, China
Production supervision by Jennifer Most Delaney
Designed by Diane M. Earley

Library of Congress Cataloging-in-Publication Data
Names: Simmons, Steven J., 1946– author. | Simmons, Clifford R., author. | Harper, Ruth E., illustrator.
Title: Where do ocean creatures sleep at night? / Steven J. Simmons and Clifford R. Simmons; illustrated by Ruth E. Harper.
Description: Watertown, MA: Charlesbridge, [2023] | Audience: Ages 3–7 years | Audience: Grades K–1 | Summary: "Learn where creatures such as a stingray, octopus, seahorse, and walrus sleep at night in informational verse." —Provided by publisher.
Identifiers: LCCN 2022056320 (print) | LCCN 2022056321 (ebook) | ISBN 9781623542979 (hardcover) | ISBN 9781632899361 (ebook)
Subjects: LCSH: Marine animals—Behavior—Juvenile literature. | Sleep behavior in animals—Juvenile literature. | Marine animals—Juvenile literature.
Classification: LCC QL122.2 .S587 2023 (print) | LCC QL122.2 (ebook) | DDC 591.77—dc23/eng/20230707
LC record available at https://lccn.loc.gov/2022056320
LC ebook record available at https://lccn.loc.gov/2022056321

Printed in China
(hc) 10 9 8 7 6 5 4 3 2 1